BETTER TOGETHER

Six Essential Conversations for Cultivating Adult SEL
and Relational Trust in Your School

Copyright 2020

All rights reserved. This book or parts thereof may not be reproduced in any form – electronic, photocopy, or otherwise – without prior written permission of the author. For permission requests, write to the author at "Attention: Permissions" at jsalazar@josalazarcoaching.org

First edition, 2020

ISBN 9798626285857

Edited and formatted by Kay Daly

Cover design and artwork by Laura Hankins

Diversity Wheel Illustration © 2016 Ades, used with permission from The Johns Hopkins Diversity Leadership Council.

Contact the author: jsalazar@josalazarcoaching.org

To Uli, who never stopped believing in this project
and pushed me forward each time I almost gave up.
We all deserve a cheerleader like you.

CONTENTS

Introduction — 1

How It Works — 9

Session 1: Collective Agreements — 15

Session 2: Stories of Us — 25

Session 3: Reflecting on Values — 35

Session 4: What Colors Your View? — 49

Session 5: Sidelining Stress — 61

Session 6: Supportive Strategies — 73

Appendices — 87

    SAMPLE: Introductory Letter to Staff — 90

    Better Together Small-Group Sample Meeting Schedule — 91

    Guidance for Collecting Data — 93

    References — 95

    For Your Notes — 98

INTRODUCTION

INTRODUCTION

Working in schools was one of the most rewarding, exciting, and uplifting jobs I've ever had. It was also one of the hardest. But the biggest challenges I experienced were not the ones you typically hear about. Yes, there were long hours, paperwork that took me away from the kids, and competing demands. But my biggest challenge was the sense that I was totally alone. I desperately wanted to be part of a community of impassioned educators, but everyone around me seemed detached and disinterested.

Years later, I've come to understand that experience. My colleagues weren't indifferent: They were burned out. Stressed. Overwhelmed. They longed for the same sense of community, of shared purpose and trust, that I craved. But they didn't have the tools, support, and workplace culture to create it.

Since that first job, I've had the opportunity to speak to thousands of educators. Working in the central office of a large urban school district, I watched teachers struggle with stress and isolation. Later, in my work with education nonprofits, I saw the same things in districts nationwide.

Here's what I learned: All over the country, educators are not connecting with one another. School staff do not know or trust one another. They compete. They fear being vulnerable with one another. Their schools don't offer a climate and culture to foster healthy staff relationships. As a result they struggle to collaborate effectively, ultimately selling our students—and themselves—short.

That's why I developed **Better Together: Six Essential Conversations for Cultivating Adult SEL and Relational Trust in Your School**. A sense of belonging is one of the most fundamental human needs. That doesn't change when we show up to work. When times get hard, when stress is at an all-time high, we need that connection more than ever. That's what this resource focuses on: concrete, hands-on, practical activities to transform schools into true *communities*.

The need is clear: **If we do not create time for educators to connect, build trust, collaborate, and be vulnerable with one another, we will lose them.** They will bounce from school to school, district to district, looking for a school that feels like home. They will leave the field and go sell insurance or cut hair. They will go back to school for a different degree. We will lose their passion for changing children's lives. We cannot afford this as a nation. Not now.

That's the central mission of **Better Together**: To give school-based educators the tools they need to build the connection they crave. It's critical for the adults working in schools and, ultimately, for the students whose lives they touch.

There is no time to lose.

© 2020. For individual use only. Photocopying is restricted.

Introduction ───────

Better Together: Six Essential Conversations for Cultivating Adult SEL and Adult Relational Trust in Your School

Each year, schools across the country are challenged to meet higher and higher standards, but lasting reform is hard to achieve, especially in high-poverty urban districts (Brewster & Railsback, 2003). While school reform is a complex and multifaceted topic, researchers Bryk and Schneider have identified a linchpin for lasting change: building relational trust. In their 2003 study, they outlined four ways that building relational trust can improve the experiences of school staff and, by extension, their students:

- **Trust lowers the sense of uncertainty and vulnerability** that comes with high stakes and heavy workloads.

- **Trust empowers all members of a school community** to unite around a plan of action and solve problems together.

- **Trust creates an environment where everyone understands expectations,** so they can work more effectively as a team with minimal supervision.

- **Trust helps schools tap and focus the common motivation of all educators**—the desire to serve students' best interest—even if that means trying new things and taking risks.

As Brewster and Railsback (2003) summarize these findings, "while trust alone does not guarantee success, schools with little or no trust have almost no chance of improving."

Better Together aims to build relational trust in schools through social and emotional learning (SEL) at the adult level. The Collaborative for Academic, Social, and Emotional Learning (CASEL) defines SEL as the process through which we acquire and effectively apply the knowledge, attitudes, and skills necessary to understand and manage emotions, set and achieve positive goals, feel and show empathy for others, establish and maintain positive relationships, and make responsible decisions (CASEL, 2020).

It takes strong social and emotional competence to be reflective, remain calm, self-advocate, be kind, be firm, form relationships, and make ethical decisions, especially when faced with the stress that comes with being an educator. But cultivating these skills is essential. Teachers with strong social and emotional competence have higher levels of trust with their peers at work (Bryk & Schneider, 2002), are more likely to demonstrate patience and empathy and encourage healthy communication (Brackett et al., 2008), and are less likely to report burnout (Brackett et al., 2010).

Teachers with strong social and emotional competencies also build and maintain stronger relationships with their students (Jennings & Greenberg, 2009). But building and strengthening these competencies takes focused time and strategic collaboration.

© 2020. For individual use only. Photocopying is restricted.

Better Together creates structured opportunities for staff to connect, share stories, and get to know one another beyond the surface level while strengthening critical social and emotional competencies like self-awareness and social awareness, with the ultimate goal of building trusting and empathetic relationships.

Introduction

Why Does My School Need *Better Together*?

Even the strongest schools can benefit from additional opportunities for staff to connect and deepen relationships. For some schools, though, there are clear red flags that indicate a need for building trust. Have you noticed any of these signs at your school?

1. **Is your staff calling in sick...a lot?** Teachers and their children get sick from time to time. It's a fact of life. When it happens, they should absolutely stay home and take excellent care of themselves and their families. However, sometimes a strange pattern of call-offs emerges. It usually happens on Mondays and Fridays and it seems to get worse toward the end of the school year. There is usually a perfectly credible excuse attached to the call-offs—"I think I have a fever" or "my child is sick" or "I have a migraine." But are you starting to wonder if those are just excuses to take a break? When a weekend to recharge isn't enough and you've started to see a pattern of lower teacher attendance, it's time to ask yourself, "Is my staff okay?"

2. **Is the rumor mill churning?** Are you overhearing staff members gossiping about one another? Are they rolling their eyes when one of their peers speaks up in a meeting? Are grade-level team meetings becoming a hostile environment? Occasional gossip is practically a fact of life, but when it becomes the norm, it's time to take action.

3. **Are staff coming to leadership to solve interpersonal issues?** When staff members are struggling to get along and work together effectively, do they talk it out and solve the problem themselves, or do they go tell the boss? When leadership is asked to solve interpersonal problems, nobody wins. The ability to address conflict requires courage, self-awareness, the ability to choose words wisely, and above all—the feeling that it is safe to confront the issue. When staff ask leadership for help, it's a good indicator that they either do not have the skills to confront the issue or that they do not feel safe doing so.

4. **Are staff losing their patience with one another? With students? With parents?** We lose our patience when we have reached the end of our coping strategies and we can't see a light at the end of the stress tunnel. Losing patience with peers, students, or students' parents damages relationships and wears away at trust. If staff are routinely losing their patience, it's time to start asking why.

5. **Was your turnover rate 20% or more last year?** When a job is too much to handle and staff don't feel supported, they quit. If they're quitting en masse, it may be an indicator that something needs to change—and fast. High turnover rates are costly both for student learning and for district budgets and should never be ignored.

6. **Have your staff stopped speaking up, sharing feedback, and voicing new ideas in meetings?** Andy Stanley said, "Leaders who don't listen will eventually be surrounded by

people who have nothing to say." When meetings are dominated by a few voices, staff will eventually shut down. Feeling disengaged, disinvested, and discouraged doesn't happen overnight. If your staff are losing steam in meetings, it's time to get help.

It's all about the students

While ***Better Together*** aims to build trust and improve collaboration among staff through adult social and emotional learning, stronger adult relationships are not the endgame; they merely set the stage for forward momentum. Creating a safe, supportive school environment where all students can thrive academically, socially, and emotionally will always be the endgame. But first, we must focus on the fundamentals, and it all starts with trust. Let's get to work!

HOW IT WORKS

HOW IT WORKS

Better Together provides school-based teams with a six-part reflection and discussion series for building trust by improving collaboration and growing the social and emotional skills of their staff.

The process

Participants are asked to prepare for each discussion session in advance by reviewing a short (1-2 page) reading and engaging in individual reflection and writing. (Preparation should take 20-30 minutes per session.) Then, the group assembles for a structured discussion about the materials they have prepared.

Through these sessions, your school offers opportunities for connection that will help form the foundation of staff relationships, stronger social and emotional skills, and a more collaborative school staff that can thrive when faced with any challenge.

Each school will move through ***Better Together*** at its own pace. You may choose to do one discussion per week, or meet less frequently depending on the time you have available. Regardless of the frequency, ensure that you develop a set schedule for group discussions beforehand. ***See the Appendix for a sample schedule.***

What this resource provides

The following six chapters provide the materials and guidance you'll need to conduct sessions on six topics:

Session 1: Collective Agreements

Session 2: Stories of Us

Session 3: Reflecting on Values

Session 4: What Colors Your View?

Session 5: Sidelining Stress

Session 6: Supportive Strategies

© 2020. For individual use only. Photocopying is restricted.

In each chapter you'll find:

A Reading to be read independently, prior to the group discussions. The reading sets the tone for the upcoming group conversations, explains the topic, and provides context for the reflection that follows.

A Reflection, including guiding questions and writing space to prepare for the group discussion. As with the reading, this independent reflection is intended to be completed before the group discussion begins.

Guidance for a Structured, Small-Group Discussion with a fully scripted set of questions to spark a reflective and productive group interaction. Each small-group discussion is broken into a **Welcome**, a **Runway Conversation** to ease participants into the session, and a **Discussion and Share-Out**, in which participants share the materials they prepared for the session. The sessions also provide an activity to **Go the Extra Mile** as an optional follow-up.

The role of the coordinator

Better Together will require at least one person to act as a coordinator to keep all staff on track. This could be a principal, assistant principal, counselor, teacher, or any staff member who is willing to dedicate the necessary time and effort. Coordinators should plan to dedicate about 30 minutes per week to their role. The coordinator does not need to be an expert in the subject matter within this discussion series. Instead, they serve as a coach, ensuring that the following tasks are completed:

- ♦ Create schedules for small-group meetings.
- ♦ Distribute materials.
- ♦ Send reminders to complete individual activities and attend small and large group activities.
- ♦ Maintain a positive and enthusiastic attitude throughout the process.
- ♦ Answer questions about the process.

© 2020. For individual use only. Photocopying is restricted.

The role of the facilitator

Each group session will require one facilitator who will keep the group moving forward, watch the clock, and ensure that the collective agreements are read aloud and followed during the session. Ask for a volunteer in advance of each session, striving to have each participant take a turn as facilitator (if possible). The designated facilitator will want to review the structured discussion prior to the session so they can anticipate the timing and needs of the discussion.

Recommendations for assembling small groups

Small groups should be composed of 4 to 8 participants. It's important to be strategic when selecting who will be in each group. Before you make a decision, consider which relationships need to grow. Do you wish grade-level teams functioned more effectively? Is there a generational or racial divide in your school? Are there specific groups who need to be able to work well together, but aren't? Ensure that you are pairing people in ways that align with their needs. Those who are paired together will grow together.

While it is preferred that a school engages in **Better Together** as a whole, it's possible to use this resource as an independent small group. For example, a single grade-level team may choose to use these discussions during their grade-level team time as a way to strengthen collaboration and grow together.

Using talking circles to structure group discussions

Throughout **Better Together**, groups are encouraged to use a **talking circle** to share stories and ensure that each member of the group has an opportunity to speak uninterrupted. With its roots in indigenous cultures, circles have been used to promote self-reflection, problem-solving, empathic listening, and the sharing of stories (Umbreit, 2003).

To use this strategy, ask the group to arrange their chairs into a circle and choose a **talking piece**. A talking piece is a small token or trinket that the speaker holds, which symbolizes that it is their turn to speak. The facilitator then poses a question to the group and invites one member to take hold of the talking piece and share their response. Once the first individual is finished sharing, they pass the talking piece to the person next to them. The talking piece is then shared around the circle until each person has had an opportunity to speak. After everyone has had a chance to speak, the talking piece can be passed again as needed to offer group members a chance to share more or follow up on a colleague's response.

© 2020. For individual use only. Photocopying is restricted.

What is the principal's role?

The principal has a critically important role in ensuring that trust is built among staff. A study by Goddard, Tschannen-Moran, and Hoy (2001) found that when teachers have opportunities to collaborate with their principal, their trust in their principal improves. A second study found that when teachers trust their principal, they're more likely to trust one another, their students, and even their students' parents (Hoy, Tschannen-Moran, 2003).

It is absolutely essential for principals to participate in **Better Together** alongside school staff, *not as observers, but as active, full participants*. By prioritizing their participation, principals communicate their commitment to improvement and acknowledge that they, too, have a role to play in building a supportive, trusting environment. While principals won't be able to attend each small group session throughout the school, they may choose to participate in one or two different groups each week. Other principals may prefer to join a single group. Either strategy can work as long as full participation is prioritized.

Data collection

Measuring the impact of **Better Together** is important for continuous improvement and can be beneficial, especially if you will need to justify the time you are spending to your district leaders or project funders.

It's common to think of data collection as something you do at the end of a process, but it's actually critical to do initial data collection at the start. By assessing adult climate and culture *before* starting the sessions, you'll be able to set a baseline. Then, when you have completed the discussion series, you can collect the same set of data to determine and demonstrate the impact of this work. **See the Appendix for guidance on data collection.**

CHAPTER 1: COLLECTIVE AGREEMENTS

CHAPTER 1: COLLECTIVE AGREEMENTS

The topic for this section is **collective agreements**. This is a set of guidelines that a group collaboratively generates to ensure that there is a shared understanding about how the group will interact during these sessions so that everyone feels safe, supported, and successful.

Goal: The group will generate their own collective agreements for future work.

In this chapter, you'll find:

A Reading to be read independently, prior to the group discussion. The reading sets the tone for the upcoming group conversations, explains the topic, and provides context for the reflection that follows.

A Reflection, including guiding questions and writing space to prepare for the group discussion. As with the reading, this independent reflection is intended to be completed before the group discussion begins.

Guidance for a Structured, Small-Group Discussion with a fully scripted set of questions to spark a reflective and productive group interaction. In this discussion, participants will work collaboratively to achieve the goal of this session.

© 2020. For individual use only. Photocopying is restricted.

Pre-Discussion Reading: Session 1—Collective Agreements

In the first small group session we will be focusing on collective agreements, which we will develop collaboratively to guide our work together. This first step is critical to the group's future work. We are all fundamentally motivated by a need to belong and form attachments with one another (Baumeister & Leary, 1995, Cacioppo & Patrick, 2008). This doesn't change when we show up to work. In fact, when we're in the kind of high-stress, high-demand environments that are so common in schools, this need to connect is amplified.

When we're operating in chaos, it's easy to let stress divide us, or worse, turn us against each other. But we can fight back against the stress and the chaos. Simply spending focused time together can help us form more favorable views of one another and even go so far as to reduce previously held biases (Wilder & Thompson, 1980; Bryk & Schneider 2003).

Collective agreements might address some of the following situations:

- How will you address disagreement or conflict?
- How will you confront racism, sexism, ageism, etc., if it arises during your sessions?
- Will you have a confidentiality agreement?
- Will you have expectations around timeliness and completion of individual work prior to each group session?
- Will you need agreements about staying engaged during sessions, active listening, honesty, etc.?

Personal conversations, frequent dialogue, shared work, and shared responsibility are the building blocks of authentic relationships (Lambert, 1998). That's why each session of **Better Together** provides school staff with structured opportunities to connect on a personal level with one another.

Connection, though, requires vulnerability, and with vulnerability comes risk. When we interact, collaborate, and open up to people we haven't previously been close to, fear is a common experience. We might find ourselves wondering, "What if a colleague betrays my trust? What if I say or do something that angers others? What if I speak honestly and I am judged? What if I am misunderstood?"

While vulnerability will always carry risk, there are ways to ensure that those risks are minimized. One way to do so is to develop a set of **collective agreements** before work begins.

Collective agreements ensure that there is a common understanding about what each member of a group will need in order to feel safe, supported, and successful. Collective agreements answer the question, "how do we all agree to interact with one another so that we can work together effectively?" Collective agreements might include statements like, "actively listen when others speak," or "when conflict arises, pause to address it courageously," or "keep conversations confidential."

Why go through the trouble to create collective agreements? Aren't we all successful adults who have been navigating social interactions for decades? **It's risky to assume that everyone knows what is expected of them, especially in a new, unfamiliar situation when we are asked to be vulnerable.** Collective agreements make everyone's expectations explicit, minimize missteps, and help build a foundation of trust.

Collective agreements are relational. They go deeper than the rules that show up in the employee handbook, which regulate things like what time to show up for work, what work must be produced, or the dress code. They allow each member of a group to share what they need in order to be a full participant a group and what it will take to feel safe participating.

Collective Agreements

Collective Agreements: Individual Reflection

1. **Think about your past small-group experiences: What went well? What could have gone better?**

2. **What kinds of collective agreements would ensure that you feel safe and supported in your small group?**

© 2020. For individual use only. Photocopying is restricted.

Collective Agreements

3. Below, write down 3-5 agreements that you would like to suggest. Then, write one or two sentences about why that specific agreement is important to you.

Example: Encourage equity of voice: Sometimes only a few voices are heard. If you notice that someone hasn't said anything for a while, I think we should offer that person an opportunity to speak.

Collective Agreements

Collective Agreements: Group Discussion
Time for completion: 60 minutes

 ### Welcome *(5 minutes)*

Facilitator: Welcome to our first group session. Today we'll start with some quick introductions. Then we'll take some time to connect and create our group's collective agreements.

 ### Runway Conversation *(10 minutes)*

What's a Runway Conversation?

Each group session will begin with a "runway conversation," which helps participants ease into the session. Typically, these questions are low-stakes and allow group members to share as much or as little as they like. Think of them as a warm-up, leading into deeper conversations.

Facilitator: We will each have an opportunity respond to questions and share out, one at a time, using a talking piece to help ensure equity of voice. When you have the talking piece, the floor is yours.

[Share the following guiding questions and discussion topics.]

1. If you have new staff or a group whose members are unfamiliar with one another, ask each participant to share their name, role, and the number of years they've been at the school.

2. Invite each member of the group to tell a brief story (1 minute or less) about their favorite day or experience at this school. Give one minute of "think time." Then use the talking piece to take turns sharing.

3. Thank the group for sharing and introduce the central activity: Creating collective agreements.

 ### Discussion and Share-Out: Collective Agreements *(25 minutes)*

Facilitator: The purpose of creating collective agreements is to ensure that the group has a shared understanding of how everyone will interact during these sessions so that we all feel safe, supported, and successful.

© 2020. For individual use only. Photocopying is restricted.

[Guide the group through the following steps to create collective agreements:]

Step 1: Invite each member of the group to take turns sharing one of the agreements they wrote down and why it's important to them. As each person shares, they will write it down on a sticky note and stick it on a wall or chart paper for all to see.

Step 2: Continue to share one agreement at a time until all members have shared their 3-5 agreements. As more and more sticky notes are placed on the wall or chart, the facilitator will begin to group the sticky notes by common themes.

Step 3: Once all the proposed agreements have been shared, the group will work to summarize, shape, and refine them until they have a list of 3-5 agreements that have been unanimously accepted.

Step 4: Ask for one or two volunteers to use their artistic skills to create a poster featuring the collective agreements that will be brought to all future group sessions.

 Checking Out *(10 minutes)*

Facilitator: *Thanks for a successful first session, everyone. We'll check out with a few closing questions.*

[Offer participants the opportunity to discuss the following questions.]

What did you learn about your group members?

What did you learn about your own needs?

What are you looking forward to most about the upcoming group sessions?

Who will volunteer to facilitate the next session?

Facilitator: *Don't forget to complete next week's reading and reflection. Let's thank our teammates and have a great rest of the day.*

Collective Agreements ⎯⎯⎯⎯⎯⎯

> ## Going the extra mile
>
>  Take your small-group collective agreements one step further by developing one set of collective agreements for the entire staff.
>
> Ask one or two volunteers to collect the agreements from each small group. The volunteers can then consolidate similar items, find common themes, and narrow the larger list down to 3-5 agreements that seem to be most important to staff.
>
> Staff can then decide what those collective agreements look like when interacting with one another, when interacting with students, and when interacting with students' families. The result is a set of collective agreements that guides all interactions.

CHAPTER 2: STORIES OF US

CHAPTER 2: STORIES OF US

The topic for this section is **storytelling** – specifically, sharing the stories of how each of us became educators. Sharing stories about ourselves is an opportunity for self-awareness and reflection. It's also a way to share our histories, understand one another's values, and build trust.

Goal: The members of the group will draft and share stories of how they became educators.

In this chapter, you'll find:

A Reading to be read independently, prior to the group discussion. The reading sets the tone for the upcoming group conversations, explains the topic, and provides context for the reflection that follows.

A Reflection, including guiding questions and writing space to prepare for the group discussion. As with the reading, this independent reflection is intended to be completed before the group discussion begins.

Guidance for a Structured, Small-Group Discussion with a fully scripted set of questions to spark a reflective and productive group interaction. In this discussion, participants will work collaboratively to achieve the goal of this session.

Pre-Discussion Reading: Session 2—Stories of Us

One of the things that makes us human is our rich tradition of storytelling. For thousands of years storytelling was how history was passed to the next generation. While stories have historical and cultural importance, they continue to be an essential part of understanding ourselves and each other.

Today, storytelling is used in organizations as a means of communicating shared norms and values, developing trust and commitment, sharing knowledge, facilitating new understandings, and building connections (Sole & Wilson, 2002). Storytelling can be especially important in situations where trust has been broken. In fact, studies in narrative therapy have found that telling and listening to stories can actually repair trust and commitment (White, 1995).

Strategies for effective reflection and writing time:
- Find a quiet space to work.
- Make sure you're hydrated and not hungry!
- Give yourself a designated amount of time that you'll spend and stick to it. Set a timer if it's helpful.
- Turn off your phone and close all email and social media windows.
- If you get stuck, call a friend or family member and try to talk it out.

In a school, perhaps the most essential story for a staff to tell is the story of why and how each person became an educator. These educator stories are always unique, but also tend to share a common thread or two. Your educator story speaks to your identity, your beliefs, and why you are who you are. These stories matter.

Storytelling is an opportunity for self-awareness and reflection. As we prepare to tell the stories of how we became educators, we naturally look back on our choices and think about the people and events that influenced us. In the end, we come away with a new understanding of who we are and an opportunity to share that inspiring story with others.

Listening to the stories of others also helps us enhance our social awareness. When we hear others' stories, we often can't help but empathize with them—and empathy is essential for trust and understanding. It humanizes. It gives us a common connection that sets the stage for cooperation and encourages us to stand up for one another, compromise when things get tough, and collaborate to share heavy workloads.

As our schools grow and become more diverse in race, gender identity, age, culture, and life experiences, it is more important than ever to ensure that we connect and share our stories with one another. Without those stories, it becomes easier to make assumptions, feed misunderstandings, and form opinions of those who are different from us. But when we share our stories, see our commonalities, and understand one another, we have an opportunity to stop seeing one another as "other."

This week, during your individual reflection time, you will write your educator story and prepare to share it with your team. As you tell your story, you will have the freedom to decide just how much detail to include, which pieces to emphasize, and which parts of your story remain yours.

Stories of Us: Individual Reflection

During our group session, you will be invited to share a five-minute version of your educator story with your small group. If it's helpful, use the guiding questions on this page to help structure your story.

> **Guiding Questions:**
>
> Why did you choose education?
>
> Who helped you along the way?
>
> What challenges did you face?
>
> When did you almost fail?
>
> What privileges and advantages did you have?

_____

_____

_____

_____

_____

_____

_____

_____

_____

_____

Stories of Us

Stories of Us: Group Discussion
Time for completion: 60-90 minutes

 Welcome (1 minute)

Facilitator: *Welcome to our second group reflection. Last time we met, we created some collective agreements to ensure that these group reflections feel safe, supportive, and effective. As we mentioned last time, we'll read these agreements at the beginning of each group session.*

[Read your group's collective agreements aloud.]

What's a Runway Conversation?

Each group session will begin with a "runway conversation," which helps participants ease into the session. Typically, these questions are low-stakes and allow group members to share as much or as little as they like. Think of them as a warm-up, leading into deeper conversations.

 Runway Conversation (5 minutes)

Facilitator: *Let's begin today with a runway conversation. We'll go around the circle and take turns responding: What was the best part of your day today? Let's all agree to spend about 30 seconds each. Who would like to go first?*

[Once everyone has shared, thank the group and move into the main topic.]

 Discussion and Share-Out: Stories of Us (5 minutes per person)

Facilitator: *During our individual reflection activity, we were all asked to write down the stories of how and why we became educators. We'll take about 5 minutes each to read our stories aloud to the group. As we each share, we'll give our full attention to the storyteller and save our questions for later in the session. After everyone has shared, we'll take some time to ask follow-up questions and reflect. Is there anyone who would be willing to share first?*

[Each member of the group takes about 5 minutes to share. If it is helpful, ask each participant to use a sand timer or their phones to monitor their own airtime. After each group member has shared, use the discussion questions to continue the conversation.]

© 2020. For individual use only. Photocopying is restricted.

Checking Out *(15-20 minutes)*

Facilitator: *Thanks for sharing, everyone. Let's take some time to think about the stories we heard. I'll ask a question, and then we can all chime in with our answers. If you have a question for the group, feel free to ask.*

[Ask the following questions to the group using a talking piece.]

- What did you learn about your colleagues that was unexpected?
- As you were writing your own story, what did you learn about yourself?
- Why was writing and sharing our stories important?
- How might our students' stories differ from ours? Why does this matter?

Facilitator: *Today, we all shared an important part of our histories with one another. We are all encouraged to continue these discussions as we have the opportunity to connect with one another. Now we'll dismiss, but before we do, let's be sure to thank one another for our contributions.*

Going the extra mile

 Take your small group storytelling one step further by hosting an after-school large-group storytelling session. This can be done in one large circle during one event, or it can become a weekly event with 5-8 individuals sharing each week.

Consider turning these storytelling sessions into an open-mic style event, inviting teachers and students to listen in as well.

CHAPTER 3: REFLECTING ON VALUES

CHAPTER 3: REFLECTING ON VALUES

The topic for this section is **reflecting on values**. Our values define our character and show up in how we treat others, how we manage difficult emotions, and many other ways.

Goal: Participants will reflect on and write about their core values, and then share them with the group as a way to build self-awareness, better understand one another, and grow relationships among the group.

In this chapter, you'll find:

A Reading to be read independently, prior to the group discussion. The reading sets the tone for the upcoming group conversations, explains the topic, and provides context for the reflection that follows.

A Reflection, including guiding questions and writing space to prepare for the group discussion. As with the reading, this independent reflection is intended to be completed before the group discussion begins.

Guidance for a Structured, Small-Group Discussion with a fully scripted set of questions to spark a reflective and productive group interaction. In this discussion, participants will work collaboratively to achieve the goal of this session.

Reflecting on Values

Pre-Discussion Reading: Session 3—Reflecting on Values

In a letter to his students in 1922, George Washington Carver laid out "eight cardinal virtues" that he hoped his students would live by:

- Be clean both inside and out.
- Neither look up to the rich nor down on the poor.
- Lose, if need be, without squealing.
- Win without bragging.
- Always be considerate of women, children, and older people.
- Be too brave to lie.
- Be too generous to cheat.
- Take your share of the world and let others take theirs.

The values that George Washington Carver shared with his students were, no doubt, shaped by a lifetime of experiences, both big and small, positive and negative. Because each of us has been shaped by our own unique experiences, it's safe to assume that, if given the task, we would each have our own unique set of values to live by.

Most people have never put pen to paper and described their values, and yet we are constantly communicating our values through our everyday behavior. They show up in big ways, like how we treat others, or how we manage difficult emotions. But they also show up in smaller ways, like deciding whether to follow through with that favor you promised, what you choose to say to a struggling colleague, or whether you will give up on a difficult task. In short, our values define our character.

Most of us adhere to our own values automatically. They are so deeply engrained in our character that we barely notice them. But noticing and naming them is important. When we are fully aware of our values, can name them, and can communicate them to others, they become a powerful resource that helps us become more self-aware.

In much the same way, when we can talk with others about their values, learn them, and work to deeply understand them, we become more socially aware and are able to form closer relationships filled with empathy and support. Knowing others' values can help us get better at assuming positive intent and be less likely to take their behavior personally. In fact, research tells us that the skill of being able to accurately interpret others' behavior and respond in socially appropriate ways decreases the likelihood of aggression and hostility between groups and individuals (Crick & Dodge, 1994).

As we identify our own values, it's important to think about the experiences that shaped each value. It's likely that our values were shaped by our heartbreaks, our challenges, our successes, and the influence of our families and role models.

This week, we'll take the time to reflect on our own values and how we acquired them. Then each of us will have the opportunity to share our stories and listen to our colleague's reflections.

Reflecting on Values

Reflecting On Values: Individual Reflection

Think carefully about the values that you live by and strive to fulfill. Then, think about where each value came from: Who influenced each value? Did you adopt them out of necessity? Did they develop as a result of a positive or negative experience? Finally, consider how these values have helped you grow and find success. How do they impact the way you bring yourself to work each day? How do they impact the way you interact with your colleagues and your students?

Use the guiding questions below to complete your independent reflection. During your group session, you'll be able to share your insights with your colleagues.

Having trouble?

To help get some ideas flowing about your values, answer the reflection prompts here:

- What do you believe about others?
- What do you believe about yourself?
- What beliefs and values drive you to be your best?
- What does success look like to you?

Value 1:

_____

_____

_____

Where did this value come from? Why is it important to you?

_____

_____

_____

© 2020. For individual use only. Photocopying is restricted.

Reflecting on Values

How does this value show up in your everyday interactions with your colleagues and students?

Value 2:

Where did this value come from? Why is it important to you?

Reflecting on Values ———————

How does this value show up in your everyday interactions with your colleagues and students?

_____
_____
_____
_____
_____
_____
_____
_____
_____

Value 3:

_____
_____

Where did this value come from? Why is it important to you?

_____
_____
_____

———————— Reflecting on Values

How does this value show up in your everyday interactions with your colleagues and students?

_____
_____
_____
_____
_____
_____
_____
_____
_____
_____

Value 4:

_____
_____

Where did this value come from? Why is it important to you?

_____
_____
_____

Reflecting on Values ─────────

How does this value show up in your everyday interactions with your colleagues and students?

_____
_____
_____
_____
_____
_____
_____
_____
_____

Value 5:

_____
_____
_____

Where did this value come from? Why is it important to you?

_____
_____
_____

———————— Reflecting on Values

How does this value show up in your everyday interactions with your colleagues and students?

Reflecting on Values ─────────

Reflecting On Values: Group Discussion
Time for completion: 60 minutes

 Welcome *(1 minute)*

Facilitator: *Welcome, everyone. Last time, we shared our educator stories. Today we're going to learn even more about each other by sharing our values. Before we begin, let's review our collective agreements. Take a moment to read them silently. As you read, think about one agreement that you want to especially focus on today.*

What's a Runway Conversation?

Each group session will begin with a "runway conversation," which helps participants ease into the session. Typically, these questions are low-stakes and allow group members to share as much or as little as they like. Think of them as a warm-up, leading into deeper conversations.

 Runway Conversation *(5 minutes)*

Facilitator: *Just like last time, we'll begin with a runway conversation that eases us into today's topic. Take a moment to share one thing you're looking forward to this weekend. Let's all agree to spend about 30 seconds each. Who would like to go first?*

[Once everyone has shared, thank the group and move into the main topic.]

 **Discussion and Share-Out: Reflecting on Values** *(3-5 minutes per person)*

Facilitator: *Each of us spent some time this week thinking about our values, how we came to have those values, and how they impact the ways we interact with others. Today we're going to take time to share those insights with each other. You can share as much or as little as you are comfortable with. Is someone willing to go first?*

[If it is helpful, ask each participant to use a sand timer or their phones to monitor their own airtime.]

© 2020. For individual use only. Photocopying is restricted.

———————— Reflecting on Values

 Checking Out *(15-20 minutes)*

Facilitator: *We learned a lot about each other today. Thank you for your willingness to share and be open with our group. Let's take some time to process what we just learned about each other and ourselves.*

[Ask the reflection questions below. If you have time, ask each person to share. If time is running short, choose a few volunteers.]

1. What kinds of "A ha!" moments did you have after completing the self-reflection?
2. How has this discussion changed the way you understand your colleagues?
3. How do your values differ from the rules you have posted in your classroom?
4. How might your values differ from your students' values?
5. How are you modeling your values through your everyday interactions with students and colleagues?

Going the extra mile

 Ask all staff to share their reflections by posting a list of values along with a photograph in a break room or staff lounge. This allows staff to be able to see what is most important to all of their colleagues, not just their group members. Use the blank template on the next page.

© 2020. For individual use only. Photocopying is restricted.

Reflecting on Values ─────────

	Name:
Place Photo Here	

My Values

1.

2.

3.

4.

5.

© 2020. For individual use only. Photocopying is restricted.

CHAPTER 4: WHAT COLORS YOUR VIEW?

CHAPTER 4: WHAT COLORS YOUR VIEW?

The topic for this section is **identity**. Your identity colors the lens through which you see and experience the world.

Goal: Group members will reflect on how their identity affects the way they experience the world and recognize the diverse perspectives within their groups.

In this chapter, you'll find:

 **A Reading** to be read independently, prior to the group discussion. The reading sets the tone for the upcoming group conversations, explains the topic, and provides context for the reflection that follows.

 **A Reflection,** including guiding questions and writing space to prepare for the group discussion. As with the reading, this independent reflection is intended to be completed before the group discussion begins.

 **Guidance for a Structured, Small-Group Discussion** with a fully scripted set of questions to spark a reflective and productive group interaction. In this discussion, participants will work collaboratively to achieve the goal of this session.

Pre-Discussion Reading: Session 4—What Colors Your View?

Your identity colors the lens through which you see and experience the world. None of us are immune to this truth.

Our identities are multifaceted and we develop them in many ways. Some parts, like race and sex, are assigned to us at birth. Other parts, like our religion and language, are shaped by the way we are raised. Some aspects of our identity depend on our environment and the opportunities available to us. But we are also in control of many parts of our identity. For example, things like our political affiliation, career, and some aspects of our physical appearance are chosen by us.

Regardless of how our identities came to be, they are an important driving force in the ways we communicate and interact with others, including our colleagues and our students. For this reason, it's important to think deeply about which parts of our identities are most influential in our lives and what impact they have on others and ourselves.

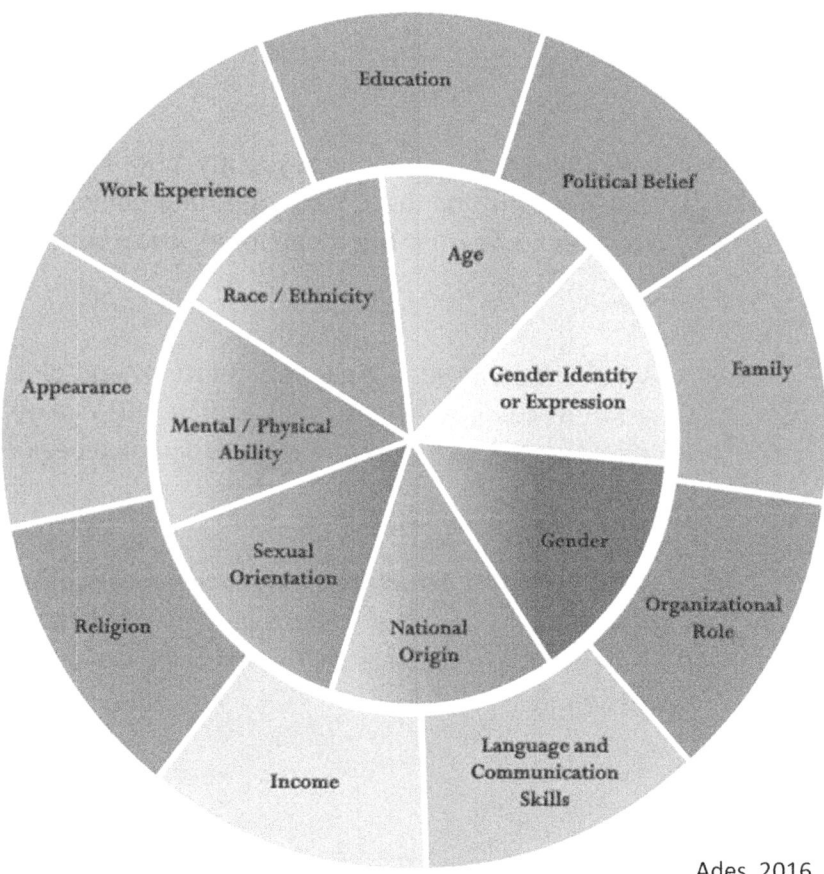

Ades, 2016

The Johns Hopkins Diversity Wheel (Ades, 2016) represents the multiple dimensions that influence our values, beliefs, behaviors, and experiences. The more permanent or visible dimensions are represented on the inside of the wheel. The outside dimensions are things that are acquired and can change throughout life, while the inside dimensions are usually stable throughout our lives. Everyone will identify more or less strongly with certain dimensions, but everyone will identify with more than one area.

We live in a world where the dimensions listed across this wheel matter a lot. When we meet a new group of people, we are most likely to trust those who share commonalities across race, gender, age, and religion (Bryk & Schneider, 2003). Put simply, we are biased in favor of those who are most like us. But as we expand the circle of individuals and groups with whom we interact, we are far less likely to let that bias influence the ways we treat each other.

In fact, when we spend focused time with others who are different from us, we can actually reduce our previously held biases (Wilder & Thompson, 1980; Bryk & Schneider, 2003; Brannon & Walton, 2013).

First, we must understand how each of the dimensions on the Johns Hopkins Diversity Wheel colors the lens through which we see the world. Through that understanding, we can more effectively put ourselves in the shoes of others and consider how these dimensions might be affecting their lives.

Privilege

As you examine your identity, remember that "privilege" is not a dirty word. If you were born into a life where privilege surrounds you, this does not mean that you have never had to struggle, nor does it mean that you have not worked hard for what you have or that you should be ashamed of having privilege. It simply means that you have had greater access to resources and/or opportunities than others, or that, because of who you are, you have faced less scrutiny by those in power. It means that you have a responsibility to acknowledge the privileges you have and use them to lift up others.

For many, examining one's identity can be uncomfortable. This is especially true for those who have grown up with identities that align with the majority (white, straight, middle class, etc.). Those who identify with the majority are rarely asked to examine their identities, primarily because their identities tend to reflect the dominant culture in educational settings, media, and entertainment.

On the other hand, those who identify with minority groups are often forced to examine their identities every day and have been marginalized, judged, and even persecuted simply for being who they are. For this reason, discussions about identity can become uncomfortable and emotional. This is okay. These uncomfortable and emotional conversations are essential for true understanding and connection. These conversations go best when participants actively listen when they are challenged to consider another point of view and when they speak the truth while also taking care to be clear and kind.

What Colors Your View?: Individual Reflection

Answer the following questions to explore your identity. During the group discussion, you will be asked to share your responses at your comfort level.

1. Which pieces of the Johns Hopkins Diversity Wheel have been most influential in shaping who you are today? (Choose 2-3 from the external domains and 2-3 of the internal domains.)

___

2. Which parts of the wheel have offered you the most safety and privilege? Why?

___

© 2020. For individual use only. Photocopying is restricted.

3. Which parts of your identity have brought challenges? Why?

4. How does your identity impact the ways you interact with your colleagues? Your students? Your students' families?

What Colors Your View?

What Colors Your View: Group Discussion
Time for completion: 60 minutes

 Welcome *(1 minute)*

Facilitator: *Welcome to our fourth session. Today we're going to talk about our identities and how they impact the ways we interact with each other. Before we dive in, let's review our shared agreements.*

[Take a moment to review your group's shared agreements.]

 **Runway Conversation** *(7 minutes)*

> ### What's a Runway Conversation?
> Each group session will begin with a "runway conversation," which helps participants ease into the session. Typically, these questions are low-stakes and allow group members to share as much or as little as they like. Think of them as a warm-up, leading into deeper conversations.

Facilitator: *Now that we're settled in, let's each take a moment to share one thing that made you smile today. Take about 15 seconds to think, and then we'll each share out.*

[Pass a talking piece around the circle and ask each team member to share one thing that made them smile today. Once everyone has shared, thank the group for their contributions.]

 **Discussion and Share-Out: What Colors Your View?** *(25 minutes)*

Facilitator: *This week we each completed a very personal individual reflection that asked us to think about the core of who we are. Because this information is very personal, you are encouraged to share as much or as little as you are comfortable with. As you are sharing personal information, ask your colleagues for confidentiality as necessary.*

To begin, let's all take turns responding to the reflection questions. I'll ask the questions one at a time. Once everyone has had an opportunity to answer the first question, we'll open the floor for questions and responses. Then, we'll move on to the next question.

© 2020. For individual use only. Photocopying is restricted.

[Ask the following questions one at a time. Use a talking piece to ensure that each participant has an opportunity to share their answers without interruption. Once each person has shared, invite the group to respond and ask questions to other group members. Then, move on to the next question.]

1. Which pieces of the Johns Hopkins Diversity Wheel were/are most influential in shaping who you are?

2. What privileges and challenges have you experienced as a result your identity?

3. How does your identity impact the ways you interact with your colleagues? Your students? Your students' families?

 Checking Out *(25 minutes)*

Facilitator: *Thank you for sharing your reflections. Let's take a moment to think about what we just heard.*

[Ask the following questions one at a time. You can either move around the circle sequentially, or allow anyone to answer.]

1. What did you learn about yourself during the individual and group reflections?

2. What did you learn about your colleagues today?

3. How did hearing from your colleagues shift your thinking?

4. How do these new understandings help us grow as a staff?

5. How does your identity differ from your students' identities? Why does this matter?

Facilitator: *Thank you for your courage and honesty today. Let's all thank our teammates and dismiss. Don't forget to complete next week's reading and reflection! See you next time.*

Going the extra mile

Discussing identify and privilege can stir strong feelings. It's possible that during your discussion, participants shared sensitive information or had strong reactions to each other's stories. It's important to honor these interactions. Each conversation brings us closer to understanding and empathizing with one another. However, if your discussions were not yet as productive as you hoped, you may decide that it's best to leave it up to individual participants about how they want to continue these discussions.

Alternately, if you had a lively and productive discussion and participants wish to continue to share and honor the elements of their identity, invite those who are so inclined to create posters highlighting the aspects of their identity they feel most connected to and share them in a communal space like a shared breakroom. It can be a fun way to provide a visual representation of what was shared in the session and continue the conversation beyond your small group.

CHAPTER 5: SIDELINING STRESS

CHAPTER 5: SIDELINING STRESS

The topic for this section is **sidelining stress**. Teaching is one of the most stressful professions in the U.S. Learning about how stress affects us and using that knowledge to help us work through it enables us to do the work we're passionate about: supporting students.

Goal: The group will reflect on, write about, and share what causes stress for them and ways to support each other.

In this chapter, you'll find:

A Reading to be read independently, prior to the group discussion. The reading sets the tone for the upcoming group conversations, explains the topic, and provides context for the reflection that follows.

A Reflection, including guiding questions and writing space to prepare for the group discussion. As with the reading, this independent reflection is intended to be completed before the group discussion begins.

Guidance for a Structured, Small-Group Discussion with a fully scripted set of questions to spark a reflective and productive group interaction. In this discussion, participants will work collaboratively to achieve the goal of this session.

Pre-Discussion Reading: Session 5—Sidelining Stress

We've all had those days where nothing seems to go our way. Maybe that lesson you planned wasn't everything you hoped it would be. Maybe you forgot your coffee at home on the kitchen counter. Maybe your students started goofing off just in time for the principal to see as she was walking past your room. Maybe you fell behind on grading last week and you are afraid you'll never catch up. These inconveniences happen to everyone, but when they are combined with federal, state, and district mandates, challenging students, less-than-perfect working conditions, family life, student debt, or any number of challenges facing educators today, life can get heavy.

Teaching has been found to be one of the most stressful professions in the U.S. (Gallup, 2014). Of course, none of us went into the field of education expecting an easy gig! Still, it's important to understand how stress affects us and use that knowledge to help us work through it, because our students are depending on us.

Stress and the body: A crash course

When we experience stress, our adrenal system releases several hormones including adrenaline, norepinephrine, and cortisol, which prepare the body for "fight or flight." This automatic stress response served us well in our hunter-gatherer days. When we saw a predator, that rush of hormones allowed oxygen to flow to our muscles, giving us enhanced speed and strength almost instantly.

But in those moments of fight or flight, our bodies have to prioritize where our energy goes. That means that while our bodies are prioritizing speed and strength, they must borrow energy from the areas that are performing non-essential functions, like the flow of oxygen to the parts of our brains that manage concentration, reasoning, decision-making, and navigating social interactions. Our primitive bodies assume that we don't need to reason, concentrate, or adhere to social standards while sprinting away from a pack of wolves.

We no longer face wild predators on a day-to-day basis. Our environment has changed drastically, but our bodies have not. To our brains, stress is still stress. Whether we're facing down a wildcat waiting to pounce or an annual evaluation, our bodies still prepare us for fight or flight. The difference is that typically, the stress we experience today doesn't require us to be faster and stronger—it requires us to think clearly and solve problems. See the dilemma? But managing stress is not out of reach. The more prepared we are to navigate challenging situations, the more likely we'll be to overcome them.

Knowing yourself

You can likely think back to a dozen experiences that caused you stress in the past week alone. You can probably remember who was involved, what happened, and how it made you feel. But have you ever taken the time to really dig in and find out exactly what triggered your stress? The answer might surprise you. When we're asked about what stresses us out, we tend to point to specific pet peeves, situations, or people, but when we look below the surface of our stress, we can see that the root cause is often more complex. David Rock (2008) has scoured the research and has identified five sources of stress in the workplace, each of which has been found to trigger that "fight or flight" response in our brains.

Five Sources of Stress in the Workplace:

1. A sense that our status is being diminished or threatened.

Examples: Fear of not measuring up to expectations. Receiving negative feedback on an evaluation. Feeling like you let someone down. Being corrected in front of your peers or your students. Being passed up for a promotion. Losing a power struggle with a student. Making a mistake. Feeling misunderstood.

2. An inability to predict what will happen in the future.

Examples: Worrying about possible budget cuts. The looming possibility of a teacher strike. Unpredictable schedules. Last-minute changes to plans. A crisis or traumatic event.

3. A lack of autonomy.

Examples: Having little control over the curriculum. Not being included in decision-making processes. Being asked to do things a rigid way. Experiencing micro-management.

4. Feeling disconnected from or unsafe with others.

Examples: Not being included in conversations. Not being invited to join others at lunch or happy hour. Not having a close friend at work. Feeling like you can't trust your coworkers. Feelings of loneliness. Experiencing a culture of gossip.

5. Experiencing or witnessing something that feels unfair.

Examples: Witnessing preferential treatment for an "in" group. Inequitable treatment of staff or students. Witnessing discrimination, bias, or prejudice. Inequitable distribution of resources.

Try thinking back to the last time you felt stressed at work. Was one of the five experiences listed above the trigger of your stress? If you dig deep enough, the answer is likely "yes."

Have you ever been at a loss for words when trying to explain what's really bothering you? Have you ever resorted to blaming your stress on an individual rather than thinking deeper about what that person triggered within you? We all have. But taking that extra step of examining your stress triggers can help prevent it from spiraling out of control. In fact, by simply recognizing and naming the root cause of our stress, we open up the possibility for change.

Putting feelings into words has been shown to slow down the fight or flight response (Lieberman et al., 2007), allowing us to think more clearly, make better decisions, and respond more easily to social cues. Alternatively, suppressing emotions can prevent us from making authentic connections with one another and has even been linked to reduced cardiovascular health (Butler & Constantine, 2005).

Being able to understand and name our stress triggers isn't just good for our health and relationships; it can help give us a language for talking through our stress, making us more likely to find a solution. When we know the source of our stress, we can explain exactly what is happening and ask others for the support that we need.

Know when to ask for help

Experiencing stress day after day is more than just inconvenient and uncomfortable. Chronic stress can have serious health effects if left untreated. Studies of high-stress helping professions found that the effects of chronic stress can include:

- Depression, emotional exhaustion, and anxiety (Radeke & Mahoney, 2000; Tyssen et al., 2001).

- Isolation, loneliness, and disrupted personal relationships (Penzer, 1984; Lushington & Luscri, 2001; Myers, 1994).

- Decreased job satisfaction and burnout (Blegen, 1993; Rosenberg & Pace, 2006).

- Reduced self-esteem (Butler & Constantine, 2005).

- Decreased ability to concentrate, reduced decision-making skills (Skosnik et al., 2000; Klein, 1996; Lehner et al., 1997).

If you are experiencing depression, anxiety, or thoughts of suicide, reach out to your employee assistance program provider, contact your doctor, seek out a mental health professional, or call the National Suicide Prevention Lifeline at 1-800-273-8255.

Sidelining Stress: Individual Reflection

Using the guiding questions below, think about the stress you have experienced at work over the past two weeks and try to identify the root cause(s). Do your best to think beyond describing events and people by using the five stress triggers on page 65 to answer the questions.

1. What were your most common stress triggers in the past two weeks? You can list things that happened at school or in your personal life.

Sidelining Stress

2. Share an example (without naming names) of a stressful situation you have experienced recently. What happened? How did it feel? What did you do? What do you wish you had done?

3. Which of the five stress triggers tend to cause you the most distress? Why?

4. Complete the following statements:

When I am stressed, my colleagues will be able to tell because…

When I'm stressed, my colleagues can help me by…

Sidelining Stress: Group Discussion
Time for completion: 60 minutes

 Welcome *(1 minute)*

Facilitator: *Welcome to our fifth session! Before we get started, let's take a moment to read through our collective agreements.*

[Show the group's collective agreements and allow time for everyone to read through them.]

 Runway Conversation *(7 minutes)*

Facilitator: *Today we're talking about something that is familiar to all of us—stress. Before we dive into the main topic, let's take a moment to share our favorite ways to de-stress. Would someone be willing to share first?*

What's a Runway Conversation?

Each group session will begin with a "runway conversation," which helps participants ease into the session. Typically, these questions are low-stakes and allow group members to share as much or as little as they like. Think of them as a warm-up, leading into deeper conversations.

 **Discussion and Share-Out: Sidelining Stress** *(25 minutes)*

Facilitator: *During your individual reflections, you were asked to think about the stress you've experienced recently and explore the root causes of that stress. Today, we'll be sharing our insights with each other. <u>As we share, let's keep in mind that we're not here to do the difficult work of problem-solving or conflict resolution</u>. Today we're just sharing our personal insights and learning about each other.*

[One by one, ask each person to share their responses to the first three questions from their individual reflections (see questions below).]

    1. What were your most common stress triggers in the past two weeks? (Use the five stress triggers on page 65 for reference.)

    2. Share an example (without naming names) of a stressful situation you have experienced recently. What happened? How did it feel? What did you do? What do you wish you had done?

    3. Which of the five stress triggers tend to cause you the most distress?

© 2020. For individual use only. Photocopying is restricted.

Facilitator: *Thank you for sharing your insights! Now that we know a little more about each other and ourselves, we can begin to ask one another for support. During your individual reflection, you were asked to complete the following statement, "When I am stressed, you'll know it because_____. My colleagues can help me by_____." Let's take a moment now to share out our responses.*

[One by one, ask each person to share their response. Encourage the group to take notes to remember the needs of their colleagues.]

 Checking Out *(25 minutes)*

Facilitator: *We heard so much honesty today. Thank you for being willing to share part of yourself with your team. Let's take a moment to think about what we just learned and what it will mean for us moving forward.*

[Ask the following questions to the group.]

1. What did you learn about yourself through this week's reflections?
2. Now that you know more about your colleagues, how will it impact your relationships?
3. How has this new knowledge changed your outlook?
4. Do our students experience these same stressors in our classrooms?
5. Can you think of a few students who might be particularly affected by the five stressors? What can you do to ease their stress?

Facilitator: *Let's thank our group members and dismiss. See you next time!*

Going the extra mile

Create a spreadsheet with the name of each staff member and their response to these prompts:

- "When I'm stressed, my colleagues will be able to tell because _____."
- "When I'm stressed, my colleagues can help me by_____."

Share the spreadsheet with the entire staff so that everyone can be thoughtful about how to provide support to their colleagues.

CHAPTER 6: SUPPORTIVE STRATEGIES

CHAPTER 6: SUPPORTIVE STRATEGIES

The topic for this section is identifying **supportive strategies** that will help us to sustain the collaborative culture we've begun to develop in these sessions.

Goal: The group will generate their top supportive strategies and create a structure to help everyone keep them top of mind.

In this chapter, you'll find:

A Reading to be read independently, prior to the group discussion. The reading sets the tone for the upcoming group conversations, explains the topic, and provides context for the reflection that follows.

A Reflection, including guiding questions and writing space to prepare for the group discussion. As with the reading, this independent reflection is intended to be completed before the group discussion begins.

Guidance for a Structured, Small-Group Discussion with a fully scripted set of questions to spark a reflective and productive group interaction. In this discussion, participants will work collaboratively to achieve the goal of this session.

Supportive Strategies

Pre-Discussion Reading: Session 6—Supportive Strategies

Over the course of our time together, we've had some important conversations. First, we worked together to establish a set of collective agreements to drive our conversations forward. Then we told one another our educator stories and shared our values. We discussed how our identities impact the way we see and interact with the world and talked about the ways that stress impacts our daily lives.

These important conversations helped us learn more about ourselves and each other. We became more self-aware and socially aware and built stronger relationships with our colleagues. Now we must ensure that these conversations have a lasting impact. Below you'll find strategies that can be used every day to keep our supportive and collaborative vibe alive.

Everyday Supportive Strategies

1. Greet each other by name. There is something special about being greeted by name. In fact, researchers wielding MRI machines have measured this! When you hear your own first name, your brain lights up in a unique way (Carmody & Lewis, 2007). Tomorrow, when you cross paths with your colleagues, trade your usual "Hi!" for a more personalized greeting.

2. Share some positive gossip. Positive gossip involves making sure that when good things are being said about someone, that person hears the good news, too. For example, if Susan tells Andre, "Last week Linda was so helpful to me. I don't know what I would have done without her!", Andre then passes that positive gossip back to Linda by telling her that Susan had nice things to say about her. Remember to only share things that are true and kind!

3. Leave a note. Have you noticed that one of your colleagues has been struggling lately? Try leaving them a supportive note. Something quick and simple will do—"You got this!" or "Slay today!" or "Good luck trying out your new lesson today! You're going to be great!" Those simple words can provide the boost they need to push through the day.

4. Lend an ear. The next time you ask, "How are you?" or "How's it going?", pause and *really* listen to the response. In most cases, you'll be surprised by how much someone will open up when you simply pause and wait for an authentic response.

© 2020. For individual use only. Photocopying is restricted.

5. Ask for advice. Did you see a colleague really shine during the last staff meeting? Do you admire the flair of their classroom decor? Do they know how to do something that you don't? Ask for their advice! Asking others for help gives them a confidence boost and helps you learn something new. As a bonus, being vulnerable enough to ask for help will encourage others open up, too.

6. Take the bulletin board challenge. The bulletin board is a school staple that has been around for decades. Today, it's practically an art form! A well-crafted bulletin board can bring joy, promote engagement, and showcase hard work. Why shouldn't staff be able to join in the fun? Staff can leverage wall space to create an interactive bulletin board where they can swap stories, share advice, and give life updates that will spark conversation and help staff stay connected with one another. Your bulletin board might feature notes of gratitude, ask staff to share their spring break plans, or provide space for staff to post a goal that they're working to achieve this year.

7. Follow through with promises. It's critically important to follow through on the promises we make to one another. The size of the promise doesn't matter. Whether it's a promise to share a resource, help a colleague with a project, or simply reply to an email, when we consistently keep our promises, we create a culture of support, responsiveness, and trust.

8. Bring snacks. This one needs no explanation. Everybody loves snacks! Go the extra mile by leaving a fun quote, an encouraging statement, or some words of gratitude next to your snack. Be sure to bring enough so that everyone can enjoy and be considerate of your colleagues' special dietary needs.

Supportive Strategies: Individual Reflection

Which of the supportive strategies do you think would have the biggest impact on your school? Why?

___

Which supportive strategy would have the biggest impact on you personally? Why?

———————— Supportive Strategies

Are there additional strategies that would be helpful to your school staff? List them here.

Supportive Strategies: Group Discussion
Time for completion: 60 minutes

 Welcome *(1 minute)*

Facilitator: *Welcome to our final session! Before we get started, let's take a moment to read through our collective agreements.*

[Show the group's collective agreements and allow time for everyone to read through them.]

 **Runway Conversation** *(5 minutes)*

What's a Runway Conversation?

Each group session will begin with a "runway conversation," which helps participants ease into the session. Typically, these questions are low-stakes and allow group members to share as much or as little as they like. Think of them as a warm-up, leading into deeper conversations.

Facilitator: *Today we're talking about the importance of feeling supported by our colleagues and how seemingly small gestures can have a big impact. Would anyone be willing to share a quick story about a time when you felt supported by a colleague?*

[Ask for 3-4 volunteers to share.]

 **Discussion and Share-Out: Supportive Strategies** *(30 minutes)*

Facilitator: *During your individual reflections, you were asked to read through a list of supportive strategies and think about the strategies that would be most impactful for our team as a whole and for you personally. Today, we are tasked with ensuring that these practices become part of our daily lives at school. First, let's share our reflections. Then we'll get to work on developing a supportive strategy for our team.*

Let's each take turns answering some questions.

[Pose the following questions, one at a time, and invite discussion of each.]

1. Which of the supportive strategies do you think will have the biggest impact on our school? Why?
2. Which supportive strategy would have the biggest impact on you personally? Why?
3. Are there additional strategies that would be helpful to our school staff?

© 2020. For individual use only. Photocopying is restricted.

Supportive Strategies

Facilitator: *Our next task is to choose a few supportive strategies that we want to become part of our everyday team culture.*

[Guide participants through the following steps, using this chart:]

	Strategy	Strategy Ambassador	Dates
1.			
2.			
3.			
4.			
5.			

Step 1: As a team, identify the top 5 strategies that you believe will make the biggest impact on your team culture. You can use some of the strategies listed in the reading or add strategies you identified in your independent reflection. Use a democratic process to vote on the top 5 strategies and list them in the chart.

Step 2: Identify 1-3 strategy ambassadors for each of the strategies. The strategy ambassadors will be responsible for ensuring that their strategy is brought to life.

Step 3: For each strategy, choose an upcoming week when that strategy will be highlighted. For example, if one of the strategies you chose was "Leave a note," you might identify the week of February 6 as "Leave a Note" week. That week, the strategy ambassadors might send an email to the team to announce the week and give them a preview of some "Leave a Note" activities that will take place. The strategy ambassador might find colorful paper and markers to share and encourage their teammates to write supportive notes to one another. The strategy ambassador would model the practice while encouraging the rest of the team to follow suit.

Step 4: Ensure that every strategy week is placed on a shared calendar. One member of the team can volunteer to remind strategy ambassadors of their strategy week, just in case! You can use the blank Support Strategy Calendars at the end of this section.

Facilitator: *Let's spend about 10-15 minutes to meet with our fellow strategy ambassadors to plan out the weeks that we identified.*

Supportive Strategies ─────────

 Checking Out *(15 minutes)*

Facilitator: *We've completed six sessions now. Let's take a moment to reflect on the conversations we've had.*

- What have you learned about yourself?

- What have you learned about your colleagues?

- How have these sessions impacted the way you think about your work?

- How have these sessions impacted the way you interact with your colleagues?

- How have these sessions impacted the way you interact with your students?

Going the extra mile

 If your school is engaged in *Better Together* as a whole, consider bringing all of the small groups together to develop a whole-school calendar of supportive strategies. Simply adapt the Group Reflection instructions to accommodate additional groups.

© 2020. For individual use only. Photocopying is restricted.

Supportive Strategy Calendar

Sun	Mon	Tue	Wed	Thu	Fri	Sat
		Notes:				

Supportive Strategies

Supportive Strategy Calendar

Sun	Mon	Tue	Wed	Thu	Fri	Sat
		Notes:				

Supportive Strategy Calendar

Sun	Mon	Tue	Wed	Thu	Fri	Sat
		Notes:				

APPENDIX

APPENDIX

- SAMPLE: Introductory Letter to Staff

- ***Better Together*** Small-Group Sample Meeting Schedule

- Guidance for Collecting Data

- References

Appendix ————————

SAMPLE: Introductory Letter to Staff

[Date]

Dear staff,

We have ambitious goals this year. **[List 2-5 of your school's primary goals here.]** In order to achieve these goals, all of us will need to work together like never before. In fact, our ability to achieve these goals is dependent on our ability to collaborate effectively as a staff.

True collaboration requires trusting relationships, deep knowledge of self, and a willingness to know and understand each other. That's why we have decided to engage in a new kind of professional learning that will help us strengthen our relationships with one another so that we can reach our goals together.

To accomplish this, we will be engaging in a series of small-group discussions over the next **[insert a timeline of your choosing]**. These discussions will take place **[insert a time or meeting structure here; e.g., during grade-level team meetings]**. Each discussion will require 20-30 minutes of individual reflection time that will need to be completed by you beforehand. You will receive a reflection workbook and weekly reminders to help us all stay on track.

Our first sessions will take place on **[dates, times, locations]**. See the attached schedule for details. I'm excited for us to begin this work together. If you have additional questions please feel free to reach out to me directly.

Thank you for your continued partnership.

[signed]

Better Together Small-Group Sample Meeting Schedule

Sample Meeting Schedule

Group Assignments:

Group A: PreK, kindergarten, and first-grade teachers, aides, and special education teachers

Group B: Second- and third-grade teachers, aides, special education and physical education

Group C: Fourth- and fifth-grade teachers, aides, special education, psychologist, and social worker

Group D: Sixth-grade teachers, aides, special education teachers, counselor, clerk, dean, principal

Group	Group Meeting Dates	Time
Session 1		
GROUP A	Wednesday, February 9, 2022	8:00 AM
GROUP B	Wednesday, February 9, 2022	9:20 AM
GROUP C	Wednesday, February 9, 2022	10:40 AM
GROUP D	Wednesday, February 9, 2022	2:35 PM
Session 2		
GROUP A	Wednesday, February 16, 2022	8:00 AM
GROUP B	Wednesday, February 16, 2022	9:20 AM
GROUP C	Wednesday, February 16, 2022	10:40 AM
GROUP D	Wednesday, February 16, 2022	2:35 PM
Session 3		
GROUP A	Wednesday, February 23, 2022	8:00 AM
GROUP B	Wednesday, February 23, 2022	9:20 AM
GROUP C	Wednesday, February 23, 2022	10:40 AM
GROUP D	Wednesday, February 23, 2022	2:35 PM
Session 4		
GROUP A	Wednesday, March 2, 2022	8:00 AM
GROUP B	Wednesday, March 2, 2022	9:20 AM
GROUP C	Wednesday, March 2, 2022	10:40 AM
GROUP D	Wednesday, March 2, 2022	2:35 PM

© 2020. For individual use only. Photocopying is restricted.

Appendix

Session 5		
GROUP A	Wednesday, March 9, 2022	8:00 AM
GROUP B	Wednesday, March 9, 2022	9:20 AM
GROUP C	Wednesday, March 9, 2022	10:40 AM
GROUP D	Wednesday, March 9, 2022	2:35 PM
Session 6		
GROUP A	Wednesday, March 16, 2022	8:00 AM
GROUP B	Wednesday, March 16, 2022	9:20 AM
GROUP C	Wednesday, March 16, 2022	10:40 AM
GROUP D	Wednesday, March 16, 2022	2:35 PM

─────────────── Appendix

Guidance for Collecting Data

Measuring the impact of *Better Together* is important for continuous improvement and can be beneficial especially if you need to justify the time you are spending to your district leaders or project funders. Here you'll find a few options for collecting both qualitative and quantitative data.

Collecting quantitative data

If you would like to measure the impact of **Better Together** using quantitative data, you can administer a survey to all staff **both before and after the project and compare the surveys to track growth**. You can use part or all of an existing survey or create a customized survey based on your school's priorities.

As you choose your survey, it's very important to ensure that staff can submit their surveys anonymously. For this reason, an online survey is always preferable. There are lots of free or low-cost online survey-building platforms that allow staff to participate anonymously and automatically generate beautiful data summary charts and graphs. These platforms include: Google Forms, Microsoft Forms, Survey Monkey, and Survey Gizmo, just to name a few.

Below you'll find a list of high-quality surveys that you can use for inspiration. You might also choose to borrow questions from these surveys to create a more customized staff survey.

- **Faculty Trust Survey**—Hoy and Tschannen-Moran (2003) developed a 26-item survey for school staff to measure trust broadly. This resource is available for free when used for scholarly purposes.

- **U Chicago 5Essentials Survey**—Many schools already complete the 5Essentials survey annually, but you don't have to wait for the annual survey administration to use the survey. You can create a custom mini-survey that can be used as a pre-post measure for *Better Together*. Be sure to focus specifically on the questions within the Collaborative Teachers and Effective Leaders domains.

- **Gallup Q12 Survey**— Gallup has studied survey results from more than 35 million employees around the world and has found that the ability to predict staff engagement centers around 12 specific questions, listed on their website. You can use some or all of these questions as a pre-post measure of your *Better Together* project.

- **US Department Of Education School Climate Survey**— The US DOE has developed a free set of School Climate surveys for multiple audiences in several different languages. Choose a few questions from their free staff surveys to design a custom pre-post survey to assess the success of your *Better Together* project.

© 2020. For individual use only. Photocopying is restricted.

Appendix ———————

Collecting qualitative data

Qualitative data brings staff voice to the forefront and can provide compelling stories of growth. As you develop your pre-post survey, add a few open-ended questions that allow for free-form text responses from staff.

References

Ades, E. (2016). *Diversity Wheel | Johns Hopkins Diversity Leadership Council*. [online] Web.jhu.edu. Available at: http://web.jhu.edu/dlc/resources/diversity_wheel/ [Accessed January 2019]. Image used with permission from the Johns Hopkins Diversity Leadership Council.

Baumeister, R.F., and M.R. Leary. (1995). "The need to belong: Desire for interpersonal attachments as a fundamental human motivation." *Psychological Bulletin,* 117, 497-529.

Blegen, M. A. (1993). Nurses' job satisfaction: A meta-analysis of related variables. *Nursing Research*, 42, 36—41.

Brackett, M.A., Katulak, N.A., Kremenitzer, J.P., Alster, B., & Caruso, D.R. (2008). Emotionally literate teaching. In M.A. Bracket, J.P. Kremenitzer, M. Maurer, M.D. Carpenter, S.E. Rivers, & N.A. Katulak (Eds.), *Emotional literacy in the classroom: Upper elementary*. Port Chester, NY: National Professional Resources.

Brackett, M.A., Palomera, R., Mojsa, J., Reyes, M., & Salovey, P. (2010). Emotion regulation ability, job satisfaction, and burnout among British secondary school teachers. *Psychology in the Schools*, 47, 406-417.

Brannon, T. N., & Walton, G. M. (2013). Enacting cultural interests: How intergroup contact reduces prejudice by sparking interest in an out-group's culture. *Psychological Science*, 24(10), 1947-1957.

Brewster, C., Railsback, J. (2003). *Building trusting relationships for school improvement: Implications for principals and teachers*. Northwest Regional Educational Laboratory.

Bryk, A.S., & Schneider, B. (2002). *Trust in schools: A core resource for improvement*. New York, NY: Russell Sage Foundation.

Bryk, A.S., & Schneider, B. (2003). Trust in schools: A core resource for school reform. *Educational Leadership*, 60(6), 40-45.

Butler, S. K., & Constantine, M. G. (2005). Collective self-esteem and burnout in professional school counselors. *Professional School Counseling*, 9, 55– 62.

Cacioppo, J.T., Patrick, W. (2008). *Loneliness: Human nature and the need for social connection.* New York: W.W. Norton & Company.

Carmody, D.P. & Lewis, M. (2007) Brain activation when hearing one's own and others' names. *Brain Res* 1116, 153-158

Appendix ———————

Collaborative for Academic, Social, and Emotional Learning. (2020, March 8). CASEL.org

Crick, N. R., & Dodge, K. A. (1994). A review and reformulation of social information-processing mechanisms in children's social adjustment. *Psychological Bulletin*, 115(1), 74-101.

Gallup (2014). *State of American schools.* Gallup, Inc.

Goddard, R.D., Tschannen-Moran, M., Hoy, W.K. (2001). A multilevel examination of the distribution and effects of teacher Trust in students and parents in urban elementary schools. The Elementary School Journal, 102 (1), 3-17. The University of Chicago Press

Hoy, W.K., & Tschannen-Moran, M. (2003). The conceptualization and measurement of faculty trust in schools: The Omnibus T-Scale. In W.K. Hoy & C.G. Miskel (Eds.), *Studies in leading and organizing schools* (pp. 181–208). Greenwich, CT: Information Age.

Jennings, P.A., & Greenberg M.T. (2009) The prosocial classroom: Teacher social and emotional competence in relation to student classroom outcomes. *Review of Educational Research*, 79(1), 491-525.

Klein, G. (1996). The effect of acute stressors on decision making. In J. Driskell & E. Salas (Eds.), *Stress and human performance* (pp. 49—88). Hillsdale, NJ: Erlbaum.

Lambert, L. (1998). *Building leadership capacity in schools*. Alexandria, VA: Association for Supervision and Curriculum Development.

Lehner, P., Seyed-Solorforough, S. M., O'Connor, M. F., Sak, S., & Mullin, T. (1997). Cognitive biases and time stress in team decision making. *IEEE Transactions on Systems, Man and Cybernetics Part A: Systems and Humans*, 27, 698 –703.

Lieberman, M.D., Eisenberger, N. I., Crockett, M.J., Tom, S.M., Pfeifer, J.H., & Way, B.M. (2007). Putting feelings into words: Affect labeling disrupts amygdala activity in response to affective stimuli. Association for Psychological Science, 18 (5) 421-427.

Lushington, K., & Luscri, G. (2001). Are counseling students stressed? A cross-cultural comparison of burnout in Australian, Singaporean and Hong Kong counseling students. *Asian Journal of Counseling*, 8, 209 –232.

Myers, M. F. (1994). *Doctors' marriages: A look at the problems and their solutions* (2nd ed.). New York: Plenum Press.

Penzer, W. N. (1984). The psychopathology of the psychotherapist. *Psychotherapy in Private Practice*, 2, 51–59.

Radeke, J. T., & Mahoney, M. J. (2000). Comparing the personal lives of psychotherapists and research psychologists. *Professional Psychology: Research and Practice*, 31, 82– 84.

© 2020. For individual use only. Photocopying is restricted.

Rock, D. (2008). SCARF: A brain-based model for collaborating with and influencing others. *NeuroLeadership Journal*. 1. 44-52.

Rosenberg, T., & Pace, M. (2006). Burnout among mental health professionals: Special considerations for the marriage and family therapist. *Journal of Marital and Family Therapy*, 32, 87–99.

Skosnik, P. D., Chatterton, R. T., & Swisher, T. (2000). Modulation of attentional inhibition by norepinephrine and cortisol after psychological stress. *International Journal of Psychophysiology*, 36, 59–68.

Sole, Deborah & Wilson, Gray. (2002). Storytelling in Organizations: The power and traps of using stories to share knowledge in organizations. LILA, Harvard, *Graduate School of Education*. 53.

Tyssen, R., Vaglum, P., Gronvold, N. T., & Ekeberg, O. (2001). Factors in medical school that predict postgraduate mental health problems in need of treatment. A nationwide and longitudinal study. *Medical Education*, 35, 110 –120.

Umbreit M. Talking circles. (2003). Minneapolis, MN: University of Minnesota, Center for Restorative Justice & Peacemaking, School of Social Work, College of Education & Human Development. Available from: www.cehd.umn.edu/ssw/rjp/resources/rj_dialogue_resources/Peacemaking_Healing_Circles/Talking_Circles.pdf.

Wilder, D. A., & Thompson, J. E. (1980). Intergroup contact with independent manipulations of in-group and out-group interaction. *Journal of Personality and Social Psychology*, 38, 589-603.

White, M. (1995). "The narrative perspective in therapy." *The Family Journal*, 2, 71-83.

For Your Notes

For Your Notes

For Your Notes

For Your Notes

About the Author

Jo Salazar is a licensed clinical social worker and organizational development professional based in Chicago. She began her career teaching social skills classes to young people in schools and quickly became interested in learning what it would take to change the culture and climate of an entire organization through social and emotional development. She has had the opportunity to do this work in organizations like Chicago Public Schools, CASEL, and Cook County Health where she has provided coaching on emotional intelligence, change management, and employee engagement. Her favorite part of this work has been helping to transform complex ideas into simple, yet practical tools that solve problems and drive improvement.

Other work by Jo A. Salazar

Leading with Emotional Intelligence:
A Daily Journal

This journal provides daily and weekly reflection practices that turn your to-do list into opportunities for growing your social and emotional intelligence in the workplace. At first glance, it might look like an organizer – but it's more than that! The reflections in this journal will challenge you to think critically about your social and emotional awareness, consider others, make decisions that are tied to larger goals, and understand how your emotions and behavior are connected. Ultimately, the reflections in this journal will become a record of your social and emotional growth at work.

© 2020. For individual use only. Photocopying is restricted.

Made in the USA
Coppell, TX
02 July 2021